Love is...

Compiled by
Olivia Warburton

Illustrated by
The Wright Sisters

LION
Giftlines

If love is the answer,
could you rephrase
the question?

Lily Tomlin

Most people experience
love without noticing
that there is anything
remarkable about it.

Boris Pasternak

What is love?

Different people will give
you different answers!
In this book you'll find
fun-sized definitions for
love-spotters everywhere
– what does love mean
to you?

I am not at all
the sort of person
you and I took me for.

Jane Carlyle

If I love you,
what does that
matter to you?

Johann Wolfgang von Goethe

There is no safety net
to protect against
attraction.

A.C. Swinburne

Come, woo me, woo me;
for now I am in a
holiday humour, and
like enough to consent.

William Shakespeare

It's very hard to get your heart and head together in life. In my case, they're not even friendly.

Woody Allen

Love can hope where reason would despair.

George, Lord Lyttleton

First love

someone special

You!

Gavin Ewart

Love is a fan club
with only two fans.

Adrian Henri

We don't believe in
rheumatism and love until
after the first attack.

Marie von Ebner-Eshcenbach

My heart has
made its mind up
And I'm afraid it's you.

Wendy Cope

Love is a
great beautifier.

Louisa May Alcott

Unrequited love

look at me

I am two fools, I know,
For loving,
and for saying so
In whining poetry.

John Donne

Love sought is good,
but given unsought
is better.

William Shakespeare

There are very few of us
who have heart enough to
be really in love without
encouragement.

Jane Austen

There is nothing like desire
for preventing the things
one says from bearing
any resemblance to what
one has in one's mind.

Marcel Proust

Wooing, so tiring.

Nancy Mitford

Crazy love

lots of fun

The human heart
likes a little disorder
in its geometry.

Louis de Bernières

In dreams and in love
there are no impossibilities.

Janos Arany

If thou remember'st not
the slightest folly
That ever love did make
thee run into,
Thou hast not loved.

William Shakespeare

You call it madness,
but I call it love.

Don Byas

I'm sending you
some kisses.
I know you like them.

Author unknown

Romantic love

lovey-dovey

One is never
too old for romance.

Ingrid Bergman

Two souls with but
a single thought,
two hearts that
beat as one.

John Keats

We all want to fall in love.
Why? Because that
experience makes us feel
completely alive. Where
every sense is heightened,
every emotion is magnified,
our everyday reality is
shattered and we are
flying into the heavens.

Author unknown

Wherever you've got
to in the tunnel of love,
remember that some
poet has been there
before you.

Daisy Goodwin

Cupboard love

need you

If thou must love me,
let it be for nought
Except for love's sake only.

Elizabeth Barrett Browning

Give me a thousand kisses,
then a hundred,
then a thousand more.

Catullus

Constant togetherness
is fine – but only
for Siamese twins.

Victoria Billings

Every man I meet
wants to protect me.
I can't figure out
from what.

Mae West

Women were brought up
to believe that men were
the answer. They weren't.
They weren't even one of
the questions.

Julian Barnes

Self love

best
ever

big
hug

one in a million

He that falls in love with himself will have no rivals.

Benjamin Franklin

Love is not self-seeking...
Love never fails.

The Bible

We had a lot
in common.
I loved him
and he loved him.

Shelley Winters

Love is mutually feeding
each other, not one living
on another like a ghoul.

Bessie Head

No woman has ever
shot her husband while
he was doing the dishes.

George Coote

Demanding love

be perfect

We do not judge
the people we love.

Jean-Paul Sartre

The difference between
friendship and love is
how much you can hurt
each other.

Ashleigh Brilliant

All love that has not
friendship for its base,
Is like a mansion
built upon the sand.

Ella Wheeler Wilcox

Relationships are like sand held in your hand. Held loosely, with an open hand, the sand remains where it is. The minute you close your hand and squeeze tightly to hold on, the sand trickles through your fingers.

Kaleel Jamison

Tug of love

to the bitter end

Love is a kind
of warfare.

Ovid

Love is the
bright foreigner,
the foreign self.

Ralph Waldo Emerson

The more I love,
the more I quarrel.

Marguerite d'Angoulème

A difference of
taste in jokes is
a great strain
on the affections.

George Eliot

I want to feel love without
making myself vulnerable.
I also want to fly and not
have to leave the ground.

K. Bradford Brown

True love

love
and
kisses

lovebirds

the one and only

True love is like
a pair of socks.
You gotta have two
and they gotta match.

Author unknown

Truly loving another
means letting go of
all expectations. It
means full acceptance.

Karen Casey

If only one could tell
true love from false love
as one can tell mushrooms
from toadstools.

Katherine Mansfield

No one is ever
betrayed by true love.

Jaufré Rudel

True love doesn't have
a happy ending: true love
doesn't have an ending.

Author unknown

Committed love

for ever and ever

Will you still love me
when I'm sixty-four?

Paul McCartney

Love is not love
that alters when
it alteration finds.

William Shakespeare

I know a lot of people
didn't expect our marriage
to last – but we've just
celebrated our two
months' anniversary.

Britt Ekland

Immature love says: 'I love you because I need you.' Mature love says: 'I need you because I love you.'

Erich Fromm

Love takes time. It needs a history of giving and receiving, laughing and crying.

Barb Upham

Unconditional love

be you

Love is unconditional...
Relationships are not.

Grant Gudmundson

Love is wanting to do
what you don't want to do
because you want to.

Mike Yaconelli

'I will love you for ever,' swears the poet. I find this easy to swear too. 'I will love you at 4.15 p.m. next Tuesday': is that still as easy?

W.H. Auden

Love rejects the question, 'What am I getting out of this?'

John Powell

Real love is a pilgrimage.
It happens when there is
no strategy, but it is very
rare because most people
are strategists.

Anita Brookner

Divine love

God smiles

Love simply IS.

Jill Harrison

To love another person
is to see the face of God.

Herbert Kretzmer

Love is the power
that heals the soul
and mends hearts.

Jill Harrison

There is no fear
in love. Perfect love
drives out fear.

The Bible

Do you want me to
tell you something
really subversive?
Love **is** everything
it's cracked up to be.
That's why people are
so cynical about it.
It really **is** worth
fighting for.

Erica Jong

To love is to risk rejection.
To live is to risk dying.
To hope is to risk despair.
To try is to risk failure.

But risks must be taken.
Because one of the
greatest dangers in life
is to risk nothing.

Only those who risk all
that they cannot keep
to gain what they can
never lose are truly free.

Simon Reynolds

To love is to receive
a glimpse of heaven.

Karen Sunde